My Little Book of Cebuano

Vol. 2

By Alfonso Borello

© Copyright 2017 Alfonso Borello
All Rights Reserved
Cover Image by Alfonso Borello
ISBN: 9781549530357

Table of Contents

Copyright
Lesson 1
Lesson 2
Lesson 3
Lesson 4
Lesson 5
Lesson 6
Lesson 7
Lesson 8
Lesson 9
Lesson 10
Lesson 11
Lesson 12
More Practice
Also by the Author
About the Author

Lesson 1

O, makahibalo ako.
Yes, I know how to speak.

O, makahibalo ko mag-Binisaya.
Yes, I know how to speak Cebuano.

O, gamay lang.
Yes, but only a little.

O, makasabot ko.
Yes, I can understand.

O, makasulti ako ug Binisaya, pero gamay lang.
Yes, I can speak Cebuano but only a little.

O, makahibalo masulti ug Binisaya.
Yes, I can speak Cebuano.

Daghan na ako ug Binisaya.
I know more Cebuano now.

Dili ako makahibalo mag Binisaya.
I don't know how speak Cebuano.

Dili ako kayo makahibalo mag Binisaya.
I don't speak Cebuano very well.

Makahibalo ako pero gamay lang.
I know but just a little.

On a separate session review the words in the cloud and try to remember the meaning. The cluster is a valuable tool for retention.

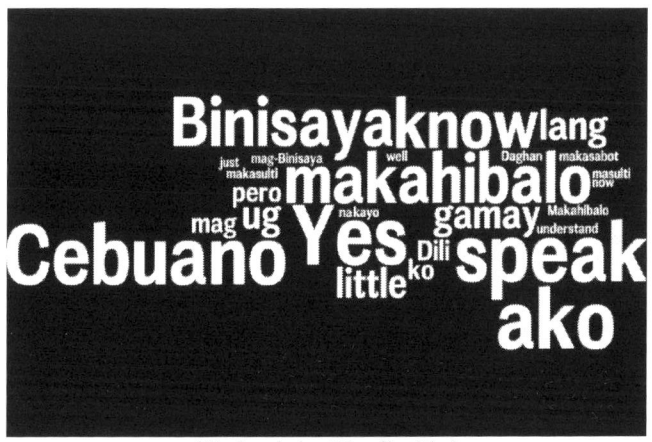

All clouds by Wordle (Tm)

Tip:

Show the written material to your Filipino friend and have her to read and record the dialogue, even just as a voice text on FB, Skype or WhatsApp.

DETAILS

Maayong buntag.

MAAYO plus the modifier NG and the noun BUNTAG.
If you see NG at the end of the adjective, it's the modifier or link.

Kumusta ka?
How are you?
KA is the pronoun, short for ikaw (you), in this case is the subject.

Ako, Ikaw, Siya (pronounced sha), can go anywhere in the sentence. The short form is Ko, Ka, Si, Ta, Mo. These can't be use at the beginning of the sentence, use them always at the end, especially for questions. Any questions can end with the word BA.

Kumusta ka ba?
Or just raise the intonation of the last word?

Asa man ka? (int. Up)
Asa ka muadto?
Where are you going?
In this case the BA is not needed because ASA (where) makes it redundant and less colloquial.

SA, means from or to.

SA: Mary Jones
i.e. SA merkado

SI, no translation, added to the subject and must be used.

Ako si Mary

Lesson 2

Makasabot ko ug gamay.
I can understand a little.

Dili ako kayo makasabot.
I don't understand very well.

Palihog, usba.
Please repeat.

Unsa?
What?

Unsa 'to?
What was that?

Kadiyot lang.
Just a moment.

Hinay-hinay lang.
Slowly please.

Unsay gisulti nimo?
What did you say?

Usa pa, hinay-hinay lang.
Just a minute, please slow down.

Gamay lang ang nahibalo-an ko nga mga pulong.
I know just a few words.

Unsa sa Cebuano ang mother?
How do you say mother in Cebuano?

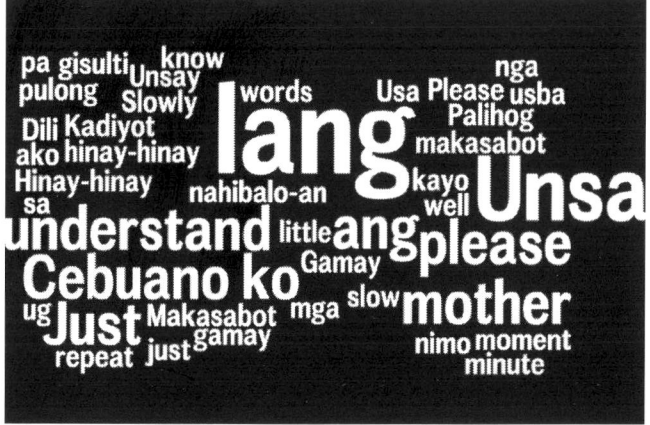

Tip:

Set your willpower to *high*. On a different session, get pen and paper and write the phrases in Bisaya/Cebuano of each lesson for maximun retention. Reach for one lesson a day.

Husto ba?
Is it correct?

Husto/sakto baa ng gisulti?
Did I say it right?

Sakto ba ang Cebuano ko?
Is my Cebuano right?

Unsa-on ko pagsulti ni ini sa Cebuano?
How do I say this in Cebuano?

Unsay angay ko isulti?
What should I say?

Dili ako makasabot sa imong gisulti.
I don't understand what you're saying.

Did you know?

Bisaya is mainly a spoken language and you will notice different spellings. i.e. Palihog or palihug.

DETAILS

Pronouns

Ako/ko: I (also adj. My)
Ikaw/ka: you, sing.
Siya: he, she (also adj. Him/her)

Kami/mi: we
Kita/ta: us
Kamo/tamo: you, plur.
Sila: they

You can use Ikaw anywhere in the sentence.
Ka is never used at the beginning.

Ako si George.
George ako.
I'm George.

Ikaw ba si George?
Usa ba ikaw George?
Are you George?

Siya Amerikano.
She's American.

Baynte dos anos siya.
She's 22.

Kami mga missionaries.
We are missionaries.

Taga-Texas sa Amerika kami.
We're from Texas, America.

Kita mga Amerikano.
We're Americans.

Mga volunteers kita.
We're volunteers.

Mga Amerikano kamo.
You're Americans.

Mga volunteers kamo.
You're volunteers.

Niabot na sila.
They have already arrived.

Kinsa sila?
Who are they?

Possessive

Nako/ko
By me

Nimo/mo
By you, sing.

Niya
By him/her

Namo, excl.
By us

Nato
By us, incl.

Ninyo
By you, pl.

Nila
By them.

Lesson 3

Nalibog ko.
I'm confused.

Nakasabot ko.
I understand.

Nalibog ko nimo.
I'm confused by you.

Nakasabot ako kanimo.
I understand you.

Nalibog ko sa imong gisulti.
I'm confused with what you're saying.

Nakasabot ko sa imong gisulti.
I understand what you're saying.

Unsay itawag niini? (also, it)
What do you call this?

Unsay ngalan niini?
What is the name of this?

Lechon kini.
It's pork.

Lechon ang itawag niini.
It's called pork.

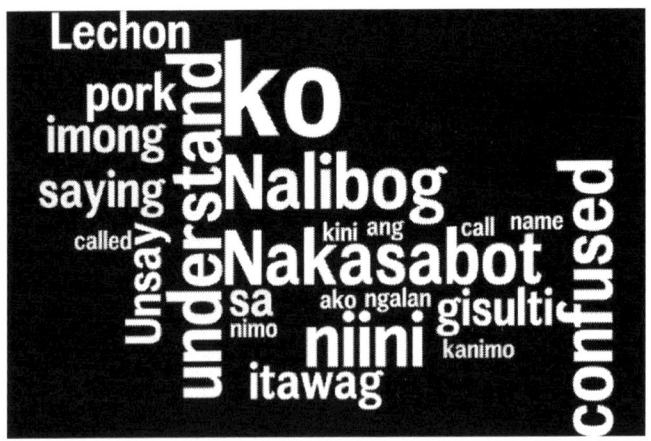

Did you know?

The Cebuano language is often referred as Bisaya, Bisayan, Binisaya, Visaya or Visayan.

DETAILS

Sometimes you have say no. Negation. This was mentioned before with the ending suffix BA.

(Negative state)
Minyo ka na ba?
Are you married?
Wala pa. Bata pa ako.

Minyo ka na ba?
Dili pa. (Just no)

Demonstrative pronouns

Naa sa Tagatay and pamilya ko. (No letter F in Cebuano, except in names)
My family is in Tagatay.

Naa sa Amerika ang akong ginikanan.
My parents are in America.

Naa sa Francia ang akong mga igsoon. (MGA pl.)
My siblings are in France.

Suffix Mo/Mu.

Motabang/Mutabang ako sa mga tawo dihni.
I'll help the people here.
(Best way to remember, think of the word ME, like 'me do this for you', foreigner like, funny but easy to recall).

The verb tabang +mo/mu. Motabang ako.

Suffix Gi.

Unsa'y klase sa trabaho ang imong gibuhat/buhaton dihni?
What type of work are you doing here?

The verb buhat + gi to emphasize that object is the focus.

Suffix On. (Again emphasis on the object on a different form).

Unsa'y imong buhaton dinhi?
What will you do here?

Lesson 4

Unsay lami?
What's the taste?

Unsay lami niana?
What does that taste like?

Tam-is kana. (adj.)
It's sweet.

Unsay lami sa pagkaon?
What's the taste of food?

Kini halang.
It's hot.

Unsa-on kini pagluto?
How is this cooked?

Gi-manteka-an.
Fried.

Gi-lung-ag.
Boiled.

Hilaw. (adj.)
Raw.

Tip:

Never try to memorize a sigle word; alway focus on entire phrases for better retention.

Lesson 5

Mas lami kung init nga isilbi.
It's better if it's served hot.

Manteka-on.
It's greasy.

Luto-on ang isda.
The fish is cooked.

Sarsado.
It has sauce in it.

Hmm…uga. Wala'y sabaw.
Hmm…dry. There's no broth.

Duna'y unod ug tambok.
There's meat and fat.

Wala'y bukog.
No bones.

Dunay mantequilla.
There's butter.

Duna'y sagol lana sa oliba. (also, a mixture)
Olive oil is added.

Unsa-on kadto pagkaon?
How do you eat that food over there?

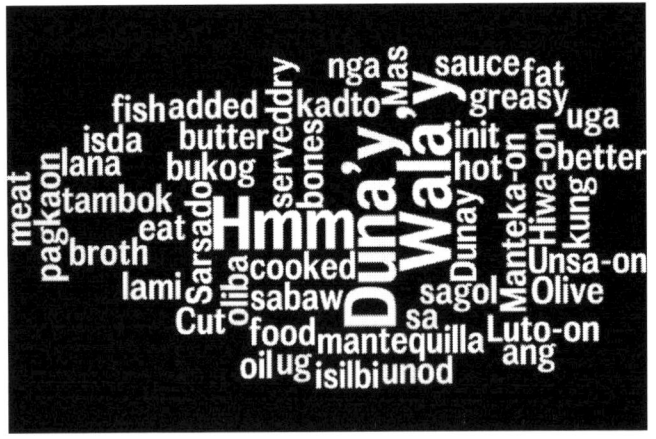

Tip:

Words separated by a dash i.e. Hiwa-on (cut it) are pronounced *legato* as one word. (*Hiwaon*) but the dash in the written phrase must be used.

Hiwa-on.
Cut it.

Kuha-on mong liso.
Remove the seeds.

Palihog, panitan.
Please peel it.

Manga-on kita.
Let's eat.

Tilawi.
Taste it.

Sige.
Ok.

Kuha ug papaya.
Get some papaya.

Did you know?

Numbers in the Philippines are often mentioned in English.

DETAILS

Personal Pronouns

Akong/ako (after a noun becomes) NAKO
My, mine

Imong/imo NIMO
Your, yours, sing.

Iyang/iya NIYA
His, her, hers

Among/amo NAMO
Ours, excl.

Atong/ato NATO
Ours, incl.

Inyong/inyo NINYO
Yours, pl.

Ilang/ila NILA
Theirs

Dako ang akong balay.
My house is big.

Guba ang imong balay. (before the noun)
Your house is destroyed.

Dako ang balay nako. (after the noun)
My house is big.

Guba ang awto nimo. (after the noun)
You car is destroyed.

More examples of before and after the noun:

Akong balay
My house
Balay nako

Imong tsinelas
Your slippers
Tsinelas nimo

Iyang lapis
His/her pencil
Lapis niya

Among balay
Our house
Balay namo

Atong leksyon
Our lesson
Leksyon nato

Inyon libro
Your book
Libro ninyo

Ilang papel
Their paper
Papel nila

Lesson 6

Gigutom ka ba?
Are you hungry?

Gusto ka bang mukaon?
Would you like to eat?

Giuhaw ka ba?
Are you thirsty?

Gusto ka ba ug mainom?
Would you like something to drink?

Unsay gusto mong kan-on?
What would you like to eat?

Gigutom ako.
I am hungry.

Unsay imong gusto?
What would you like?

Gusto ko ug pizza.
I like pizza.

Gusto kong muinom ug Lambanog.
I'd like to drink Lambanog.

Unsay naa niini?
What's in this? (also, what's the matter?)

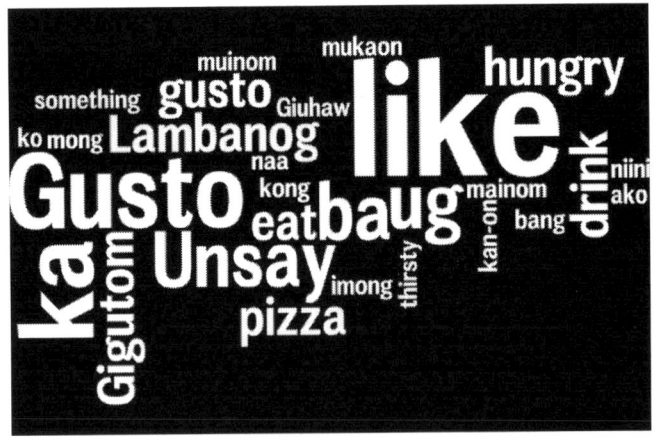

Did you know?

In Bisaya, women have the tendency to lower their pitch at the end of the sentence, while men raise their pitch, almost as they were to ask a question.

DETAILS

Demonstrative pronouns review:

Unsa'y imong trabaho dinhi?
What's your job here.

Unsa'y imong buhaton dinhi sa Pilipinas?
What will you do here in the Philippines?

TAGA, indicating from (place) go first for emphasis. To make it easier to remember, what you hear in a question first, you shall use first in the response.

Taga diin ka?
From where are you?

Argentina ako.
I'm from Argentina.

No so for the the word BA at the end for asking questions.

Minyo ka na ba?
Are you married?

Dili pa.
No. PA means still and it's used often for emphasis.

Ulitawa pa ako.
I'm still single.

Masakit pa ako.
I'm still sick.

Wala pa.
Non yet.

Wala pa, bata pa ako.
Non yet, I'm still young.

Let's review the prounouns

Ako, ko
Siya.
Sila.

Possessive pronouns.

Unsa'y/Kinsa imong ngalan? (The g in the NG is silent it's pronounced NA).
What's your name?

Pila'y imong edad?
What's your age?

Naa sa Manila ang aking ginikanan. (GI is pronounced like in the word GEAR)
My parents are from Manila.

                Personal pronouns.

Niya.
Nimo.
Nila.

Albert ang ngalang niya. (Y is silent).
His name is Albert.

James ug John ang ngalan nila. (UG pronounced ah with a glottal stop).
Their name is James and John.

Unsa'y angga nimo?
What' your nickname?

About Unsa and Asa. What and where can also be used as Which.

Kinsa'y imong ngalan?
What's your name?

Asa ka nagpuyo?
Where do you live?

Pila and imong igsoon? (SOON pronounced SO-ON).
How many sisters or brothers do you have?

Pila'y edas sa imong amahan ug inahan?
How old are your father and mother?

Markers in Bisaya/Cebuano.

Sa: at/in/on/with
Ang: the
Para: for
Pinaagi sa: through

Lesson 7

Unsay mga sagol niini?
What are the ingredients in this dish?

Unsay imong gigamit?
What did you use? (also, what are you using?)

Duna ba kini ug kamati?
Does it have tomaotes?

Unsay imong gipangita?
What are you looking for?

Unsay imong gikinahanglan?
What do you need?

Unsay inyong gusto?
What do you want?

Mopalit ako ug gatas.
I will buy some milk. (also, I buy milk)

Papalit ko sa inyong bugas.
Let me buy some rice. (also, I'll get you some rice)

Duna ba mo'y pancit?
Do you have noodles?

Mahimong mutan-aw sa saging ninyo?
Can I see your bananas?

Gusto unta ko nga mopalit mga patatas.
I'd like to buy some potatoes.

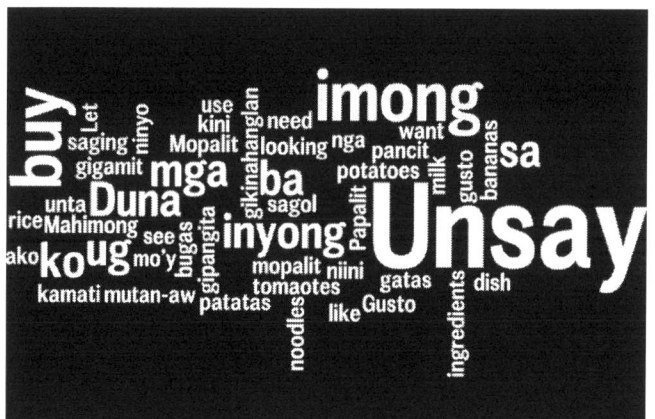

DETAILS

Difference between ANG and ANG MGA.

Ang is singular.
Ang mga (pronounced ma-ha) is plural.

Pila na ang imong edad?
How old are you? (lit. What's your age?)

Pila na ang mga edad nila karon?
How old are they now?

The prefix I. Used to indicate the thing or object used to perform the action.

Unsa'y itawag nimo? (tawag, verb + i).
How do they call you?

The affix NAG. (In the present tense, now. Later we shall see the difference with the affix MAG, in the near future).

Asa ka nagpuyo sa Amerika?
Where do you live in America?

Asa ka nagtrabaho? (Nag + verb trabaho)
Where do you work?

Lesson 8

Unsay gidak-on?
What size?

Unsay kolor ang gusto nimo?
What color do you like?

Duna ba'y pula nga? (nga, pron.: na-ha)
Do you have red? (also, is there any red?)

Asa ang mga kamatis?
Where are the tomatoes?

Duna ba mo'y mga karot niini?
Do you have carrots?

Tagpila?
How much?

Tagpila ang kilo ka?
How much is a kilo?

Duna ba'y makapalit nga sagi?
Where can one buy bananas?

Duna ba'y tindahan sa kamati dinhi?
Is there a store here which sells tomatoes?

Didto lang.
Over there.

Tingali sa City Market.
Maybe at the city market.

Dinha dapit.
Toward that direction.

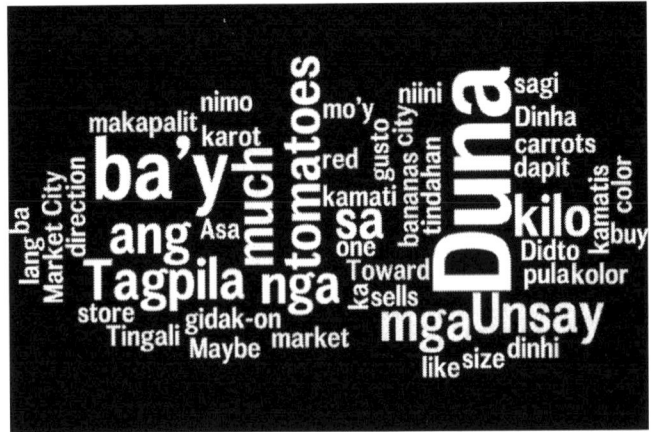

Did you know?

Most Filipinos speak a sentence with a combination of Tagalog, Bisaya, Ilongo, Chavacano (broken Spanish), and English words; even on national media. It can be frustrated, but it also helps a little if you are learning the language. If you're communicating a very important issue, make sure they understand, and put it in writing, because they will say yes just to please you, even if English is the legalese. Lawyers are no exception, and often, amusingly indeed, you must amend their writing.

DETAILS

More Possessive Pron.

Ako
Mine, my

Imo
Your, sing.

Iya
His/hers

Amo
Our/ours, excl.

Ato
Our/ours, incl.

Inyo
You/yours, pl.

Ila
Their/theirs

Some Examples:

Akong libro
My book

Akong lapis
My pencil

Iyang awto (aw pron: au)
His car

Iyang mama
Her mother

Among baboy
Out pig

Among tanom
Out plants

Atong tindahan
Our store

Atong barangay
Our neighborhood center

Inyon balay
Your house

Inyon bintana
Your window

Ilang simbahan
Their church

Ilang butang
Their things

Lesson 9

100 pesos lang.
Only 100 pesos.

Para nimo, 90 na lang.
For you, just 90 pesos.

Sus, kamahal!
Gee! How expensive.

Sobra kamahal!
Too expensive!

Kamahal sa imong baliya!
Your goods are too expensive!

Makahangyo ba?
Is a discount possible?

Sige na, 85 pesos na lang kini. (also, kini)
C'mon, 85 pesos for this one.

Pahangyo-a 'ta bi?
Discount, please? (also, bargain)

Dili mahimo.
It's not possible.

Dili na mahimo nga mamenosan.
It's not possible for the price to be reduced.

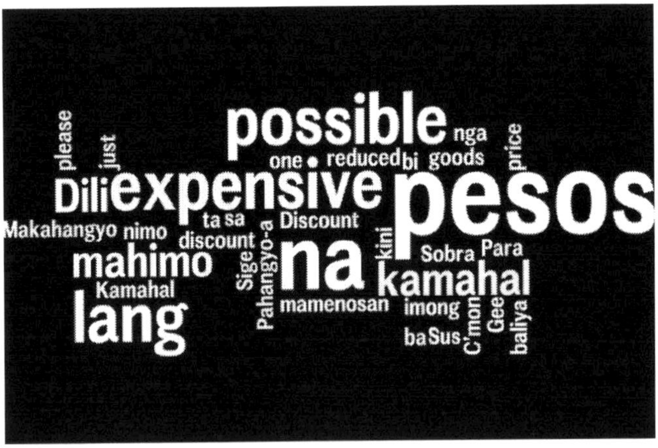
possible
please
just
nga
price
one
reduced
bi
goods
Dili
expensive
pesos
ta sa
Discount
Makahangyo
nimo
discount
kini
Sobra
Para
mahimo
Sige
Pahangyo-a
na
kamahal
Kamahal
mamenosan
imong
lang
Gee
ba
Sus
C'mon
baliya

Lesson 10

Wala na'y hangyo, ma-alkanse ko.
There's no discount, there won't be any profit left.

Kung dili nimo menosan, dili na lang ko mopalit.
If you won't reduce the price, I won't buy anymore.

Mutan-aw una ko sa uban.
I'll look around first.

Sige na lang.
All right.

Sige, para Buena mano.
Alright, a special price for the first customer.

Sige, basta ikaw.
Okay, as long as it's you.

Kamahal, sige na lang.
It's expensive, never mind.

Mahal kayo. Dili na lang ko.
It's expensive, I won't make any purchase.

Bayad, o.
Here's my payment.

Nia ang akong bayad, salamat.
Here's my payment, thank you.

Sukli nako?
My change?

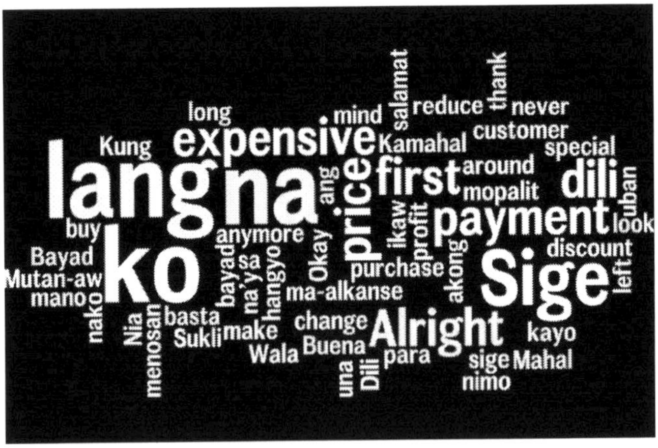
salamat
thank
long
mind
reduce
never
customer
Kung
expensive
Kamahal
special
lang
na
ang
price
first
around
dili
mopalit
uban
payment
buy
anymore
ikaw
profit
look
Bayad
ko
Okay
akong
discount
Mutan-aw
bayad
sa
purchase
Sige
left
mano
na'y
hangyo
ma-alkanse
nako
Nia
basta
change
Alright
menosan
Sukli
make
kayo
Wala
Buena
para
una
Dili
sige
Mahal
nimo

Kulang ang sukli.
There's not enough change.

Resibo ha.
The receipt.

Asa ang resibo?
Where is the receipt?

Mahimo ba nga hatagan mo ako ug resibo?
Could you please give me a receipt?

Nia, a.
Here it is.

Nia ang imong resibo.
Here is your receipt.

Nia ang resibo sa imong napalit.
Here's your receipt for the goods you've bought.

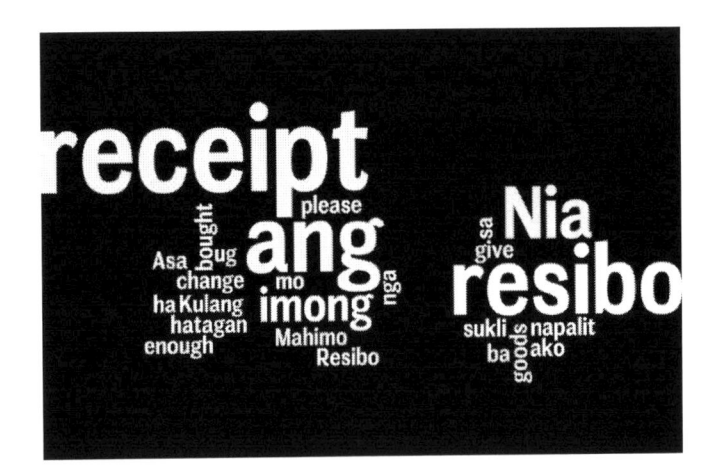

receipt please ang Nia resibo
Asa bought ug sa give
ha change mo nga
Kulang imong
hatagan Mahimo sukli napalit
enough Resibo ba goods ako

DETAILS

Demontrative Pronouns

Dali, kini ang kwarto nimo.
Come, here in the room.

Kini ang kwarto nimo.
This is your room.

Time Prepositions

Daghan kami ug kuha kada adlaw.
We have a good catch every day.

Kada Lunes.
Every Monday.

For the past we shall use niaging.

Niaging Lunes.
The previous Monday.

Niaging usang.
Before/the other.

Niaging usang Lunes.
The other Monday.

For the future we'll use sa.

Sa Lunes.
On Monday.

Sa sunod.
Next.

Sa sunod na Lunes.
Next Monday.

Review The Direction Prep.

Sa tuo.
To the right.

Sa wala.
To the left.

Sa luyod/likod.
At the back.

Review The Verb Affixes
(Gi, Mag, Nag, Mu/Mo, Na, Ni/Mi)

Gikapoy ka ba sa imong biyake?
Are you tired from your trip?

Magdugay ka ba dinhi?
Will you be here long?

Diin ka nag-tuon ug Binisaya?
Where did you learn Cebuano?

Kinsa ang nag tudlo nimo?
Who taught you?

Asa ka nagputo?
Where did you live?

Asa ka magbuyo?
Where did you live/stay?

Init ba sab didto?
Does it also get hot there?

Unsa'y imong nahuman?
What course did you finish in college?

Kanus-a ka niabut dinhi sa Pilipinas?
When did you arrive here in the Phillippines?

Let's Move Onto The Affix Maka (Action Not Yet Begun, Abililty Mood, Possibility Occurence)

Makasulti kaba ug Binisaya/Cebuano? (Maka+v. Sulti)
Can you speak Cebuano?

Makahibalo ka ba nga muBinisaya? (Maka+v. Hibalo)
Did you know how to speak Cebuano?

Makasabot ka ba ug Binisaya? (Maka+ v. Sabot)
Can you understand Cebuano?

Affix Na-An
(Ability Or Possibility)

Daghan ka bang nakat-onan sa Binisaya? (Na+v. Kat-on).
Have you learned much Cebuano already?

Affix Gi-An
(Denotes Past Action)

Kinsang pamilyaha ang imong gipuy an dinhi? (Gi+v. Puyo+An).
Which family are you staying with here?

Unsang imong gitun-an sa kolehiyo? (Gi+v. Yuon).
What did you study in college?

Intensifiers
(Kaayo)

Maayo kaayo.
It was just fine.

Kapoy kaayo.
It was tiring.

Bata pa kaayo ako.
I'm still very young.

Dato kaayo sila.
They are very rich.

Lesson 11

Gusto kong muadto sa merkado.
I'd like to go to the market.

Unsay akong sakyan?
What will I take?

Unsay maayong sakyan padulong city hall?
What's the best type of transportation going to city hall?

Mag ka tricycle.
Take the tricycle.

Magsakay ka ug pedicab.
Take the pedicab.

Wala'y pedicab didto. Kinahanglan mag dyipni.
There's no pedicab here, so you need to take the jeepney.

Asa ako musakay?
Where do i get the ride?
Where will i be able to get a ride?

Asa maayong mag-atang ug sakyanan dinhli?
Where's the best place to wait for a ride here?

Asa ang istasyon sa dyipni?
Where' the jeepney station?

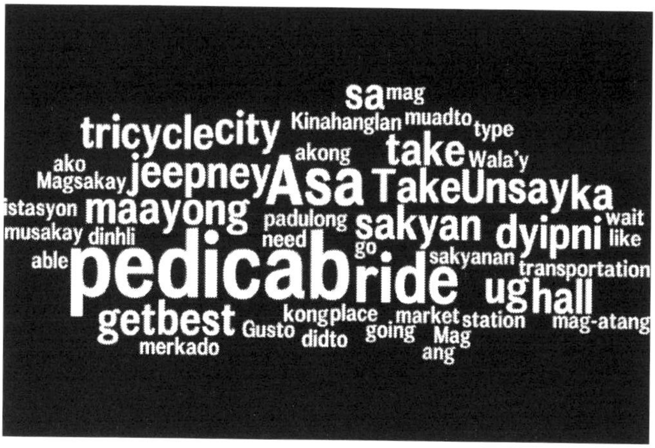
sa
mag
tricycle
city
Kinahanglan
muadto
type
akong
take
Wala'y
ako
Magsakay
jeepney
Asa
Take
Unsayka
istasyon
maayong
padulong
sakyan
dyipni
wait
musakay
dinhli
need
go
like
able
pedicab
ride
sakyanan
transportation
ug
hall
get
best
Gusto
kong
place
market
station
mag-atang
didto
going
Mag
merkado
ang

Lesson 12

Asa ako makasakay ug dyipni dinhi?
Where will I be able to get a jeepney here?

Sa lungsod.
In town.

Unahan sa city jail.
Farther ahead the city jail.

Duol sa Western.
Near the Western Union.

Sa tuo palenke.
To the right of the market.

Wala sa iglesia.
Left of the church.

Asa 'ni muagi?
Where does this vehicle pass?

Muagi ba kini sa iglesia?
Will this pass by the church?

Unsay agi-an niini?
What route does this vehicle take?

Pilay plite?
How much is the fare?

Pilay plite sa ciudad?
How much is the fare to town?

Word Cloud

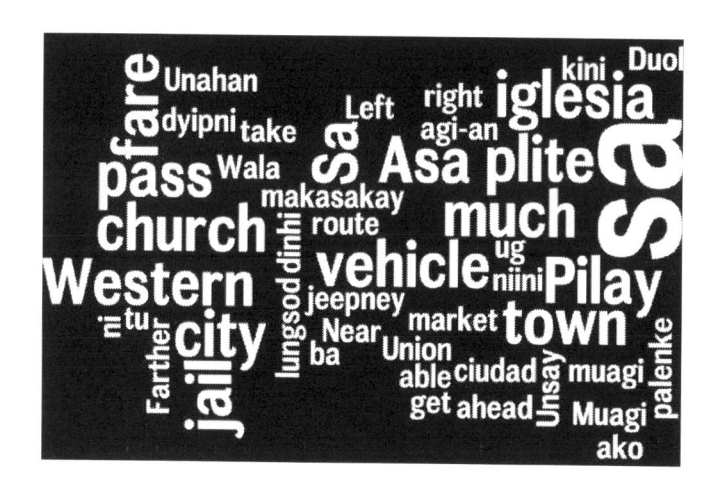

fare Unahan kini Duol
dyipni take Left right iglesia
pass Wala sa agi-an Asa plite sa
church makasakay much
route vehicle ug Pilay
Western jeepney niini
ni tu Near market town
Farther lungsod dinhi
jail city ba Union able ciudad muagi palenke
get ahead Unsay Muagi
ako

Pila'y plite hangtud sa LTO?
How much is the fare to the land and trasportation office?

Sukli nako, palihog.
My change please.

Noy, ang akong sukli, palihog.
My change please.

Asa lo man-ug?
Where do I get off?

Asa ko man-ug sa port road?
Where will i get off on port road?

Dinhi/didto lang.
Just here/there.

Sa eskina lang.
At the corner.

Para!
Stop!

Lugar lang.
To the side.

Para dinhi/dinha.
Stop right here/there.

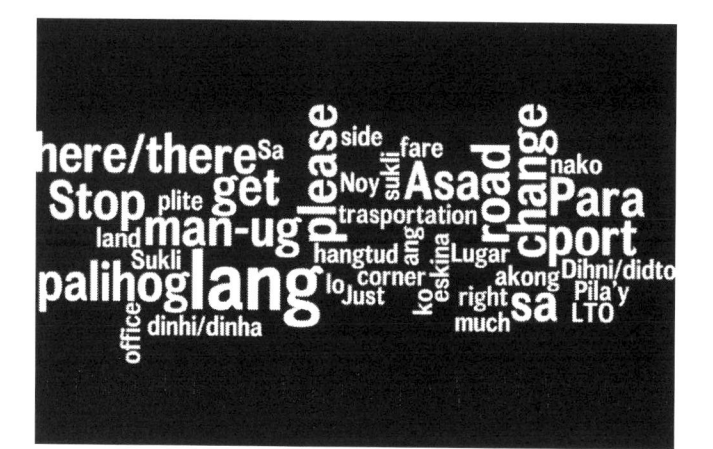

here/there Sa side fare nako
Stop plite get Noy sukli Asa road change Para
land man-ug please trasportation port
Sukli hangtud ang Lugar eskina akong Dihni/didto
palihog lang, lo Just ko corner right sa Pila'y
office dinhi/dinha much LTO

DETAILS

Connector/Conjunctions

The conjuction ug.

Kugihan si Peter.
Peter is hardworking.
Brayt si Carmen. (Sometimes you hear matalino, Tagalog, orig.)
Carmen is intelligent.

In this case we'll use a coordinating conjuction.
Kugihan ug brayt si Carmen.
Carmen is hardworking and intelligent.

The affix na. Used for a state of being or a past action attached to the verb

Nalipay ako. (Na + verb lipay).
I'm happy.

Natulog ako. (Na + verb tulog).
I'm sleeping.

The affix pag is attached to the verb used as request or command

Kumusta ang paguma? (pag+verb uma)
How's the farming?

Kumusta ang paghubi ng hayop? (pag+verb hubi)
How's animal raising?

More Practice

Unsay kahimtang sa imong negosyo?
What is your business situation?

Unsay sakit sa imong balay?
What's wrong with your home?

Unsay tanan naka agi ana?
What's going on here?

Delikado umanong sakyan.
It is dangerous to ride.

Magsakay ka ug barko.
Take a boat.

Wala'y pedicab didto.
There is no pedicab there.

Mag ka bus.
Take a bus.

Kami muadto dito ingun nga evacuate.
We are here to evacuate.

Muadto sila sa menteryo.
They go to the cemetery.

Dato kaayo nimo.
You're so rich.

Maayo kaayo.
Very good.

Si Isagani wala makasabot.
Isagani does not understand.

Kanus-a ka niabut?
When did you come?

Sa likod ng trak.
Behind the truck.

Malapit sa monumento.
Near the monument.

Dali sa kwarto.
Come in the room.

Para sa imong napalit.
For your purchase.

Mahimo ba kami nga moreklamo?
Can we complain?

Basta ikaw nalang ang kumausap.
Just as you talk.

Dili na lang ko mopalit.
I will not buy anymore.

Unsay inyong gusto?
What do you want?

Unsay imong gikinahanglan?
What do you need?

Unsay imong gipangita?
What are you looking for?

Unsay imong gigamit?
What do you use?

Nagpuyo ubos.
Living below.

Asa ka nagpuyo?
Where did you live?

Pila'y imong edad?
How old are you?

Wala pa gihapoy klaro.
It's still not clear.

Wala pa sa isip ko.
I have no idea yet.

Wala pa, bata pa ako.
No, I'm still young.

Taga diin diay ka?
Where are you?

Unsa'y imong buhaton dinhi sa Pilipinas?
What do you do here in the Philippines?

Unsa'y imong trabaho dinhi?
What's your job here?

Unsa gusto mong kan-on?
What do you want to eat?

Giuhaw ka ba?
Are you thirsty?

Gigutom ka ba?
Are you hungry?

Ang papel ay para.
The paper is for.

Daghan mga papel ug mga basahon.
Many papers and books.

Papel de liha.
Sandpaper.

Atong leksyon.
Our lesson.

Mas gusto mga tsinelas.
Prefer slippers.

Mas gusto ito.
Prefer it.

Ang mga kuaderno namo.
Our notebooks.

Ang manok niya.
Her chicken.

Ang balay nimo.
Your house.

Ang libro nako.
My book.

Asa ang pagkaon?
Where is the food?

Unsa nga klase nga negosyo?
What kind of business?

Motabang ako sa mga tawo dihni.
I will help people in this area.

Ang pamilya ko.
My family.

Minyo ka na ba?
Are you married?

Unsa ngalan niini?
What is its name?

Nalibog ko unsa akong gamiton ugma.
I was confused about what I was going to use tomorrow.

Nalibog ko ku unsa'y atong buhaton.
I'm confused about what to do.

Nakasabot ko sa imong gisulti.
I know what you say.

Dili ako makasabot sa imong gisulti.
I can not understand what you are saying.

Angay ba nga tabangan?
Should it help?

Unsay angay ko isulti?
What should I say?

Unsa-on ko pagsulti niini sa Bisaya?
How do I say this in Bisaya?

Sakto ba ang Ingles ko?
Is my English okay?

Sakto ba?
Is that right?

Husto ba?
Is it right?

Nahibalo ako.
I know it.

Unsay gisulti nimo?
What do you say?

Hinay-hinay lang.
Just slowly.

Kadiyot lang, Kinsa man.
Just for a moment, whoever.

Unsa?
What?

Asa ka muadto?
Where are you going?

Kumusta ka?
How are you?

Maayong buntag.
Good morning.

Makasulti ako ug Binisaya, pero gamay lang.
I can speak with Binisaya, but it's just a bit.

Gamay lang.
Just a little.

O, makahibalo ako.
Oh, I know it.

Kumusta ang panahon?
How is the weather?

Magtulog kami.
We sleep.

Nalipay ako.
I'm happy.

Maayo kaayo.
Very good.

Dinha.
There.

Dinhi lang.
Just here.

Sa eskina lang.
Just in the corner.

Pilay ang pasahe?
How much is the fare?

Unahan sa tindahan.
Forward to the store.

Duol sa City Hall.
Near City Hall.

Sa lungsod.
In the city.

Sige na lang.
Just go ahead.

Kung dili nimo...
If you do not...

Gikapoy ka ba?
Are you tired?

Sa likod.
On the back.

Sa tuo.
On the right.

Sa sunod na Sabado.
Next Saturday.

Sa sunod.
Next time.

Sa Lunes.
On Monday.

Kada Lunes.
Every Monday.

Kada adlaw.
Every day.

Kini ang kwarto nimo.
This is your room.

Nia ang resibo sa imong napalit.
Here is the receipt of your purchase.

Nia ang imong resibo.
Here is your receipt.

Also by the Author

Miniature Life
Signorina
Giallo
Manstat
Faceless
Bonbon
Arms Around You
The Ducati Girl
Terror in Atlanta
Let's Get into The Weird
Sorry but I Must Kill You
The Ducati Girl's Confessions
The Pillow Book of Carmen Garcia
Supercitizens
The First Party
The Ducati Girl – Family Affair
Are Popes Really Needed?
War of the Currents
The Ducati Girl, Darwin, and the Pig of Nebraska
M–Could You Be on Another Dimension?
Gramsci
The Ducati Girl: Toxic Connection
Sulla Pelle dei Poveri
Affari di Famiglia
Il Banchetto

About the Author

Multiple genres author Alfonso Borello has written drama, thrillers, travel diaries, biographies and essays on history, religion, philosophy, psychology, evolution, cosmos, revolutionaries, inventors, and numerous books on language learning in Italian, Spanish, Chinese, Tagalog, Cebuano and Thai.

Printed in Great Britain
by Amazon